I want to thank all the DIAMAN Team for the support to the realization of this eBook that I hope will help to make as many people as possible aware of the enormous opportunity that the Crypts are reserving us at this moment.

Index

PREMISE	4
CHAPTER 1 – WHY CRYPTO WILL CHANGE THE WORLD	**6**
1. A NEW TECHNOLOGY THAT WILL CHANGE THE WORLD	6
2. THE SCARCITY VALUE	8
3. ETHEREUM, THE MOTHER OF ALL CRYPTOCURRENCIES	11
4. PRICE AND VALUE ARE NOT ASSOCIATED	15
5. ASSET TOKENIZATION	19
6. THE MARKET MOVES IN BUBBLES	23
7. THE MONTE CARLO SIMULATION APPLIED TO BITCOIN	36
CHAPTER 2 – WHY INVEST CRYPTO ASSETS PROFESSIONALLY	**46**
PREFACE: INVESTING IN CRYPTO ASSETS	46
8. THE ADVANTAGE OF QUANTITATIVE MODELS	49
9. MARKET TIMING WITH CRYPTO	54
10. WHY DIAMAN STARTS WITH AN ADVANTAGE	61
11. BACKTEST AND REAL TRACK RECORD	63
12. THE IMPORTANCE OF LIQUIDITY	66

13.	CORRELATIONS BETWEEN ASSET CLASSES	68
14.	INVEST WITH HOMEOPATHIC DOSES	70
CONCLUSIONS		**74**
BIBLIOGRAPHY		**75**
DISCLAIMER		**76**
BIOGRAPHY		**77**

PREMISE

The purpose of this e-book is to introduce the fascinating world of cryptocurrencies to those who are familiar with them, though not at a technical or investor level. Our intention is not to create an exhaustive document, let alone a perfect one, as highly technical topics often require simplification to the detriment of precision.

We are speaking, in fact, of a very young topic and technology. Like a 10-year old child, crypto is still unripe and premature. It clearly requires a period of growth and refinement to broaden its scale.

To give an overused yet reliable example, ten years after the birth of the internet, connecting to it still required a modem (think back to 14.4 kbps!) that needed activation using a traditional phone line attached to a computer. The computer enabled the modem to emit crackling sounds before finally connecting to the network.

Those who lived through the early 90s surely remember the difficulties of connecting to the internet, along with the time required to load a simple webpage.

Today, most of us have smartphones that almost always automatically connect to a network, providing us with access to the world of information and applications in a very user-friendly and instant way.

However, cryptocurrencies haven't reached that level of sophisticated simplicity. If I want to buy crypto today, I need to understand public and private keys, register a seed phrase, learn to use two-factor authentication, and be proficient with a crypto trading platform.

In short, investing in cryptocurrencies is currently anything but simple.

Yet, more and more people in the world are entering this system, both in hopes to earn as well as owing to belief in the technology. Reading this little e-book will better your understanding of the crypto phenomenon and can serve to substantiate your future investment decisions.

CHAPTER 1 – WHY CRYPTO WILL CHANGE THE WORLD

1. A NEW TECHNOLOGY THAT WILL CHANGE THE WORLD

Let's suppose for a moment that time travel is possible and step into the year 2029. Not a far cry from reality, as we find ourselves in a world where wealth is more distributed, there is no longer a great disparity between the mega-rich and the remaining population. Of course, the mega-rich exist and remain very powerful, but there is also a new social class, the mega *well-to-do*, who are neither mega-rich nor "just" wealthy.

I am not talking about restoring the alleged middle class, which would still exist, but I'm speaking of a new social class in society, of people who are in possession of a few million euros and can live a more than decent lifestyle that is full of satisfaction.

The world still has wealth disparity although, after centuries in history, a new social class will have been formed comprised of people who have seized the ground-breaking occasion of technological and cultural revolution.

Theft no longer exists or is at least be limited to small micro-crimes of objects of little value. That's because communities will be interconnected through the ownership of *tokenized objects* (we will dive deeper into this topic later). Community co-ownership of tokenized objects makes theft useless without also owning the linked token. The world is more efficient and less bureaucratic, all records (like land registries, digital identities, corporate registrations, etc.) are on distributed blockchains.

In any case, are you interested in being a part of the *mega-wealthy* category in 2029?

Having the chance to do so is simple: just invest in cryptocurrencies today. If the technology takes hold, and I can assure you that it will, in ten years, you too will belong to the mega-wealthy. You don't have to invest all your assets. Instead, invest a maximum of 10% of your assets if you are over 40 and 20% if you're younger. Crypto is a high risk and very volatile investment, but if this scenario comes true, the only way to take advantage of it is by investing now (if you haven't already done so, of course).

2. THE SCARCITY VALUE

Many of you are aware that Bitcoin was originally conceived by Satoshi Nakamoto, whose origins are unknown. According to the original Bitcoin whitepaper, Bitcoin was created as a secure system of money transfer between people without the need for intermediaries.

Allow me to explain: If today you wished to transfer a sum of money from one account to another, the transfer would take place under the responsibility of the bank where you opened the account. Not seeking the help of a bank exposes you to enormous risks of fraud, unless you were to use the blockchain's distributed ledger technology.

Without getting too technical, Bitcoin was designed to remunerate the people who keep this register by logging their transactions securely.

Picture 1 – The Bitcoin Symbol composed of numbers

There's another interesting element: Bitcoin can grow infinitely in price. That's not immediately clear to ordinary people who still wonder why Bitcoin is worth $10,000. Bitcoin was designed to reach a value of hundreds of millions of dollars — do you know why? Because a Bitcoin has eight numbers behind the comma and the smallest amount of a bitcoin is actually a satoshi, or rather, 0.00000001.

Imagine if one day, a satoshi was equivalent to one US dollar, or even two or three. Then, a bitcoin would be worth $10,000,000. BTC won't hit that value now of course. The road will be long and full of many bubbles we will have to resist. Only the bravest and most tenacious will succeed in this enterprise, which is normal in the history of financial markets. Not much changes other than the exasperation behind the volatility.

Why will Bitcoin reach that value? Because at the end of its generation cycle, there will only be 21 million BTC in existence, and there are seven billion people in the world. It's the phenomenon of *scarcity*: even though we're used to inflation and increasing amounts of money printed by central banks, in crypto, this phenomenon does not exist. Some cryptocurrencies, such as the PHI token, are designed to decrease the number of tokens in circulation over time.

Scarcity, combined with increasing crypto diffusion, is the main reason why BTC price tends to rise and will continue to do so over time. Owning an entire bitcoin will be a luxury that only a few will be able to afford. At best, a few million people (while the first million remains firmly deposited in Satoshi's wallet) will own an entire bitcoin.

It's also possible this scenario will never come true — there's always that risk, but this is the most probable one I know of to become really rich in (relatively) a few years.

A small handful of people have already become millionaires thanks to cryptos (about 200,000 in the world) and won't have to wait 'til 2029...

3. ETHEREUM, THE MOTHER OF ALL CRYPTOCURRENCIES

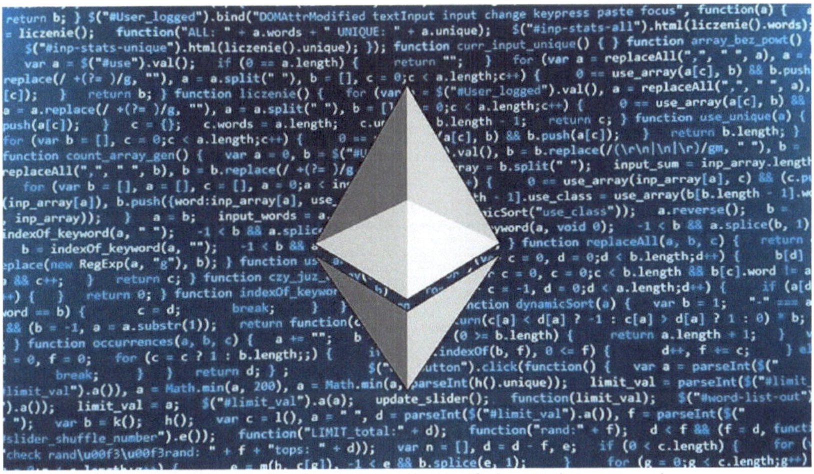

Picture 2 – A Representation of the Ethereum logo

If we were to hypothetically label Bitcoin as the *father* of blockchain, certainly Ethereum would represent the *mother* of all cryptocurrencies. Perhaps this is what the mythical prodigal son, Vitalik Buterin, thought when he imagined and created the Ethereum logo.

For those who are familiar with sacred symbols, the creator's mother is represented by the symbol known as *vesica piscis*.

the vesica piscis

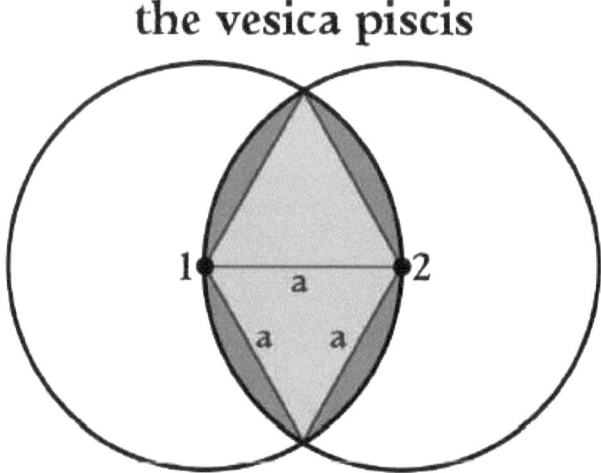

Picture 3 – The geometrical representation of vesica piscis

More specifically, the crossing of two circles (symbol of duplication) with the triangle at the center (symbol of reproduction). This might sound irreverent, but if you were to take a deeper look into sacred symbols, you might discover incredibly exciting things.

When I came across the vesica piscis, I understood just how ahead of their time Vitalik Buterin and his team were in the decision to use it as a logo.

A simple logo, seemingly without any logical sense, incorporates a powerful message: Ethereum is the mother of creation, the creation of thousands of tokens populating the universe of crypto assets.

Right, the universe. How does the universe play into all of this?

The name has its reasons, as we can see from a post by Vitalik himself in 2014, right before the crowdsale:

VitalikButerin · Administrator · Posts: 84 · admin
March 2014

I was browsing a list of elements from science fiction on Wikipedia when I came across the name. I immediately realized that I liked it better than all of the other alternatives that I had seen; I suppose it was the fact that sounded nice and it had the word "ether", referring to the hypothetical invisible medium that permeates the universe and allows light to travel.

Picture 4 – A Vitalik Buterin Tweet about the name Ether

Ether, as all physicists know, is the physical space in the seemingly empty universe that isn't actually that empty, because it allows light to pass through. Therefore, ether is something invisible that enables us to transmit a fundamental element for the spreading of life.

This is what Ethereum is. It's a fundamental element for the crypto asset ecosystem which accounts for the birth, existence, and proliferation of digital tokens and coins that are revolutionizing our way of thinking about the economy and wealth management.

There are quite a few Bitcoin extremists, with all due respect of course, who consider Bitcoin to be the only legitimate cryptocurrency. They contend that all other tokens are dangerous scams without a right to exist.

Altcoins, aka crypto assets other than Bitcoin, really *are* scams. Yet there are so many other initiatives, such as Ethereum, who have proven to have enormous value, perhaps even superior to Bitcoin, along with demonstrated and impressive potential to change the world.

Honestly, I have yet to figure out if these extremists feel this way because they see Bitcoin as the only safe option (their main weapon of attack against other cryptos), or if they hide a deeper sense of envy towards the Ethereum phenomenon, which, separate from Bitcoin, has succeeded in creating a possibly even more disruptive ecosystem.

Ethereum has managed to create a parallel universe to Bitcoin that now feeds itself, creating value for millions of people. And I'm not just talking about how compared to its conception, its value has grown tens of thousands of times. I'm referring to the whole ecosystem of developers, communication, and industry experts who work daily and gain profits from this new digital economy.

Smart contracts, invented and developed by Vitalik, can also be generated using Bitcoin, but the stroke of genius was to make them easy to create and accessible by a much wider community of developers. Those very developers created ad-hoc programming languages that are now considered standard in the community.

These same smart contracts give birth to human creativity, providing an opportunity to those with valuable ideas to transform them into projects that, if funded by the community, can, in turn, be made into reality.

Smart contracts will change the business world on multiple levels, making it more reliable, safe, and transparent. These developments will as a result improve the environment in which we live.

4. PRICE AND VALUE ARE NOT ASSOCIATED

Up to now, the vast majority of issued cryptocurrencies have been utility tokens. A utility token comes with rights and privileges of non-corporate nature and are not considered securities.

While traveling to blockchain conferences around the world, I've analyzed the different ways of using utility tokens.

Picture 5 – Utility tokens are classified as digital tokens

UTILITY

Some use them to identify a work of art, some use them to benefit economically from the energy produced by a power plant, and there are those who use them as a reward for mining a new blockchain (there are hundreds of alternative Blockchains to the Bitcoin one).

Others, like us, may use them as currency to purchase investments or professional services at a discount with respect to fiat currencies, such as the euro.

The main characteristic of the utility token is that it can be exchanged through one or more exchanges, allowing the price to fluctuate based on supply and demand.

DEMOCRATIC

This instrument allows one to buy a very low-value token, as has been happening the last few months, to then purchase goods with it when its value has increased. Therefore, I can now afford more expensive goods at a lower price, often at an additional discount compared to their value in fiat (at least this is the case in the openPHIntech.com marketplace).

As a practical example, imagine you want to buy an informational newsletter on the stock market that features a selection of the best securities and quantitative methods. This monthly newsletter is created by DIAMAN, and costs €1000 per year. On the openPHIntech marketplace, you can either pay for the newsletter with €1000, or use the PHI Token at a 30% discount, saving yourself €300 in the process.

You can then go to an exchange and purchase the corresponding €700 in PHI tokens. To simplify, let's suppose the token is valued at €.10.

At this point, 7000 PHI tokens have been delivered to DIAMAN (though it could be any other service provider, since the platform is open to third parties), and you proceed to enjoy your newsletter service for a year.

At the end of the first year, you want to renew the newsletter because the content was excellent and useful for your work, so you decide to go back on the exchange and purchase more PHI tokens to take advantage of the 30% off on your renewal.

The token is now valued at €1 because more and more people bought the PHI token to receive discounts. You buy €700 worth of PHI tokens and deliver them to DIAMAN, who in turn provides you with their service for a second year.

Now, to complete our reasoning, let's suppose that in the third year, the price has risen to €10, therefore you only need to buy 70 PHI tokens, which you deliver to DIAMAN, who in turn provides you with their service still valued at €1000.

To those who have purchased the service, the price of the PHI token was completely indifferent, since they always bought the value they needed and passed it onto DIAMAN.

For DIAMAN however, things are quite different. In three years, DIAMAN received 7770 PHI tokens, which, if sold immediately would have yielded € 2100 (aka the discounted value of the service for three years), but since DIAMAN kept the tokens, they now amount to €77,700. Not too shabby for a newsletter.

I chose this example to give you an understanding of how extraordinary a utility token can be if well managed.

It grants the less fortunate a chance to access goods or services at a reasonable price they may not have otherwise been able to afford and purchase a token that has growth potential should they wait for it to grow. Buyers have the option to save and sellers have the option to recover the applied discount with interest.

Clearly, in order to function, this whole mechanism needs growing users and a limited number of tokens. Or, in the case of the PHI token, for the number of tokens in circulation to decrease over time.

For those who are interested in reading the PHI token whitepaper, you can do so on the website www.phitoken.io.

5. ASSET TOKENIZATION

One of the biggest revolutions of the blockchain is the tokenization of assets.

WHAT DOES THIS MEAN?

The ability to issue alphanumeric data strings, combined with the ability of the blockchain to create an unmodifiable and shared register, allows the ownership of a given asset to be assigned to whoever possesses both the public and the private key.

This already happens for crypto assets. For example, if you have a bitcoin in your wallet, the technology that attests to your ownership is based on the public key (wallet address) and the private key, which is unique to the content within your specific wallet.

Picture 6 – An example of a company logo active in the tokenization business

Whether you have a bitcoin or a string that certifies your possession of a painting, it's practically the same thing.

In very open states, for example, the Cayman Islands, companies that tokenize assets of various kinds are starting to spread. Companies like Blackmoon, whom I've had the pleasure of meeting, are tokenizing American hedge funds.

You may be wondering what the sense in that is. Well, allow me to explain.

Tokenizing a hedge fund has enormous advantages.

A) I can buy a token tied 1:1 with the hedge fund's NAV share at any time, not just once a month, and without waiting months to redeem it.
B) I can trade the token tied to the fund with other people.
C) The shares of the fund are in my wallet, without expensive bank deposits.
D) I can access at lower minimum rates (the best funds often ask for a minimum of one million euros to enter) by splitting the quota with other retail investors.
E) The token is, in fact, a secondary market of the hedge fund similar to ETFs, but traded on a crypto exchange.

Clearly, the transition to a tokenized civilization won't happen quickly, and the reason for that is quite intuitive.

Let's take an example. If I want to have a token that certifies the possession of my car (today, I own a paper certificate and registration to the public registry – an entity that generates monstrous costs for the state) I'd have to convince the Italian State (or any other state) to dismiss a large part of public car registry employees and replace them with a blockchain.

There would be great savings which could be applied to many sectors, but there are social aspects to this change that need to be taken into consideration.

In June of 2018, the possession of 49% of a painting by Andy Warhol, which is shown in the figure below, was tokenized, so I'm not talking about future illusions — I'm talking about the present.

Picture 7 – A tokenized painting

In 2018, a building in New York was tokenized, and the tokens related to their possession in shares were sold in a short period of time, opening up a new frontier for the use of tokens. Think, for example, about timeshare apartments. They can achieve so much liquidity with this technology — liquidity that breathes new life into an asset of this type.

One thing is for certain! Tokenization is radically changing the world. So, the choice is yours: Stay at the border and enter only when there ise a bubble, or start getting involved to understand how the benefits of this mechanism work both in financial and cultural terms.

6. THE MARKET MOVES IN BUBBLES

Picture 8 – The Bitcoin logo inside a bubble

In the last few months (or years), there's been a lot of talk about the bond market bubble in newspapers, specialized television shows, and by elusive macro economists of the world, because more than one third of the world's debt has negative interest rates.

It is a contradiction, in financial terms, to have to pay someone to lend money, even if this person is your state. We're experiencing an absurd situation that has never happened before in the financial markets.

The main cause of negative interest rate is linked to the enormous liquidity introduced into the markets mainly by the FED, European Central Bank, and the Central Bank of Japan.

On the other hand, Keynes' famous phrase is none other than, "The market can stay irrational longer than you can stay solvent."

In reality, this absurdity is what has made it possible to avoid a failure of the financial system, therefore all the better, even though it obviously feeds irrational phenomena such as bond markets with negative yields, and stock markets that reach new highs day after day.

A phenomenon that's not actually fed by central bank money, which everyone labels as a nonsensical mega bubble, is represented by Bitcoin and cryptocurrencies.

The price of bitcoin has gone from the highs of over 18K in December 2017, coinciding with the launch of the BTC futures by the CBOE and CME, to a minimum of about 3K in 2018, losing over 80% of its value.

Is this a representation of a bubble bursting? Yes.

Does it represent the end of Bitcoin? Certainly not!

As always, I'd like to address this problem in the most analytical way possible. For this reason, I've reported a post below that I wrote shortly before the explosion of the bubble in 2017-2018. We will then draw some conclusions together on the phenomenon of financial bubbles.

Let's start with a graph:

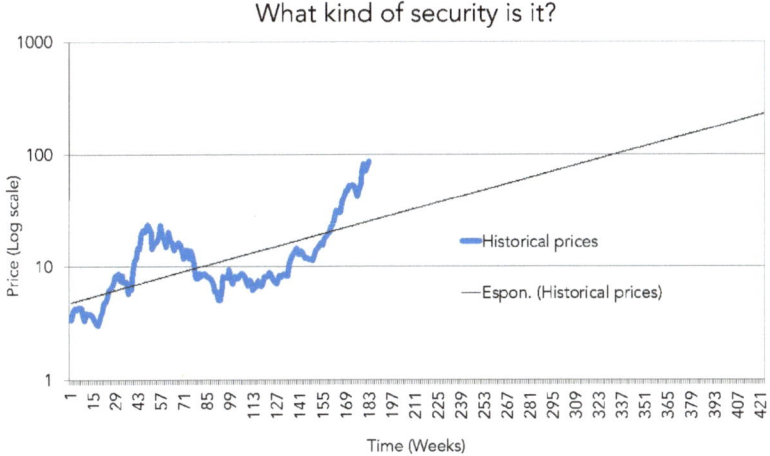

Picture 9 – An example of historical stock price

What type of security (financial instrument) does this represent? Bitcoin? Looks similar, right?

Actually, it's not. it's a Nasdaq company from the Venture Capital CMGI fund, which at the time invested in many Nasdaq technology companies. I remember that in 1999, I used it as an example because a person who had invested $1000 in 1996 had $1,000,000 by '99, a return never seen before in the financial markets.

The growth of the graph doesn't seem so striking because it's on a logarithmic scale, but in practice, it's illustrating a stock that went from $3 to almost $100 in less than three years.

But it's not over yet, that graph I showed you goes up to 1998, when in reality the company grew again, as shown in the following graph:

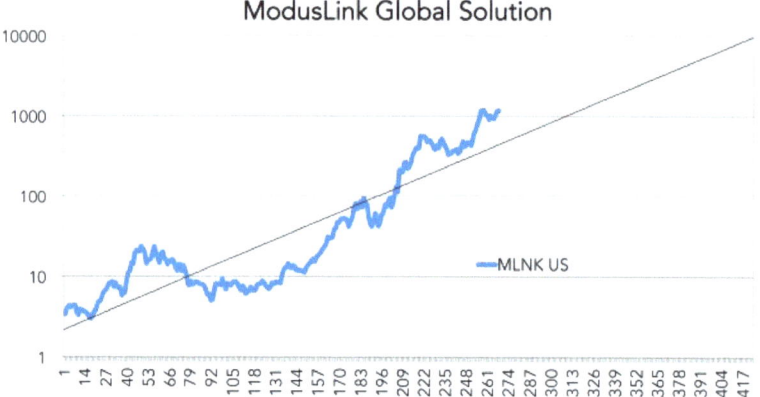

Picture 10 – Exponential growth of MLNK US (former CMGI US)

From $100, it reached a thousand in relatively little time (less than two years), which should make us pause at whoever screams miracle (or heresy) when we see the Bitcoin price rise by 1000% in a year. Wouldn't it be interesting to compare Bitcoin trends in recent years with this graph?

Picture 11 – Bitcoin compared to MLNK

Interesting right?

We cannot say that the graphs are the same, but there is in fact a similarity. To capture it, we used logarithmic graphs, as linear graphs would have excessively flattened initial values.

So, can we say that, given CMGI was the golden stock of the 2000 bubble, that Bitcoin will be the bubble of the year 2017? Or 2020? Or 2025?

Who can confirm this?

We'd have to resort to science, and this time not statistical or financial science, but science linked to the prediction of earthquakes.

A HAND FROM ACADEMIA

You'll think I've gone crazy, but... let's turn to Prof. Didier Sornette, whom I had the pleasure of meeting at Global Derivatives in Budapest in 2016. The good professor works at ETH, University of Zurich's renowned Department of Physics for earthquake prediction. Thanks to Prof. Sornette, we have a great deal of literature on forecasting financial bubbles, including mathematical models and practical examples which you can find on the ETH website.

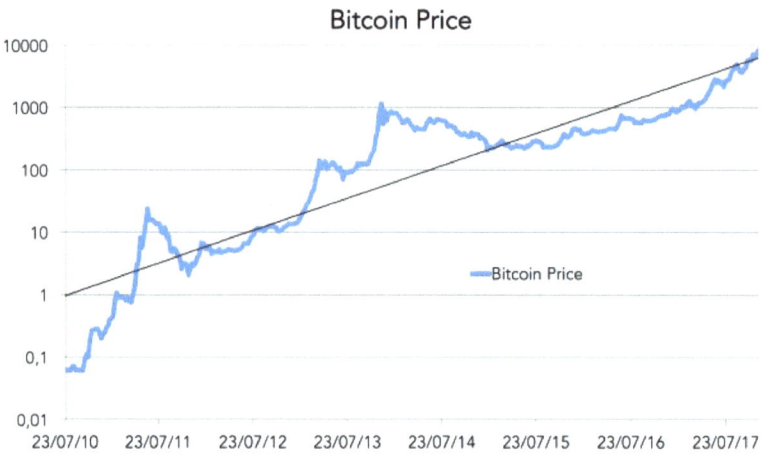

Picture 12 – Bitcoin price and exponential linear regression (log scale)

One of the clearest signs that a financial market is in a bubble is the exponential growth in prices. When a bubble becomes unsustainable, it bursts like a soap bubble and vaporizes the savings of the latest arrivals, who typically pay for all the others who've made a profit.

HOW THE LOGARITHMIC SCALE WORKS

To translate this into a comprehensible message, in a logarithmic graph like the one above, the line represents an exponential growth, so if the market grows faster than this line, it means the market's growth is higher than exponential growth and is unsustainable in the long run.

As you can see from the graph, however, the historical series of Bitcoin in the first phase of its life had an even higher growth rate than its current one, which suggests that in reality it is outlining a growth that is (albeit incredible for the increase rates) sustainable.

CLARITY

Attention, this doesn't mean that I'm claiming a Bitcoin crisis is impossible and won't happen, far from it. I believe that sooner or later there will be a cryptocurrency crisis that will purify the market from the numerous ICOs that have taken advantage of the moment to drain liquidity from the system without a clear growth prospect.

IT'S NOT ALL FLUFF

Here too, don't get me wrong. There are companies that have raised a lot of money and will probably go on to become successful in the future. But as it so happens in the world of start-ups, there's always been a very high mortality rate (I know something about this, unfortunately….). It is certain that even twenty years ago with the New Economy bubble, there were companies that took advantage of the moment to raise money that they would never have collected any other way (Pets.com should ring a bell).

But, back to Bitcoin and us — is it in a bubble, or not?

It's true that the growth rate of this period has returned to being slightly above exponential, but it's supported by a demographic growth of users (still few) who are entering this world, estimated at around 18 million, and equal to a little more than 0.2% of the world population.

USERS

With a little effort, I found the graphs relating to the number of active wallets, which may not exactly correspond to the number of people owning one because many, including myself, have more than one open and working wallet. In any case, since it's very difficult to have exact numbers, with the understanding that not all wallets were included in the analysis, we'll have to accept it as an adequate estimate.

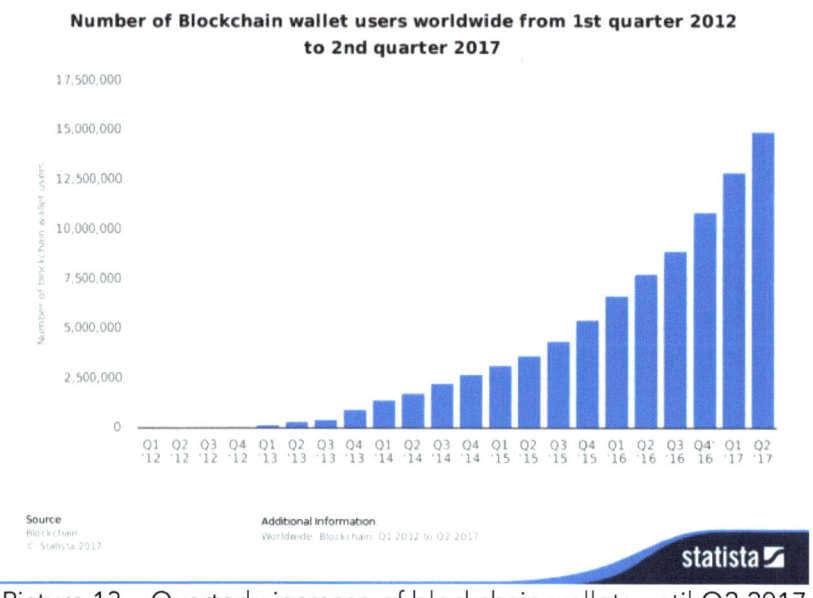

Picture 13 – Quarterly increase of blockchain wallets until Q2 2017

Above is the first graph about the demographic growth of users in the world of cryptocurrencies.

INCREDIBLE

I then tried to insert the growth of the number of wallets (in logarithmic scale of course) in comparison bitcoin price, and discovered a very interesting relationship.

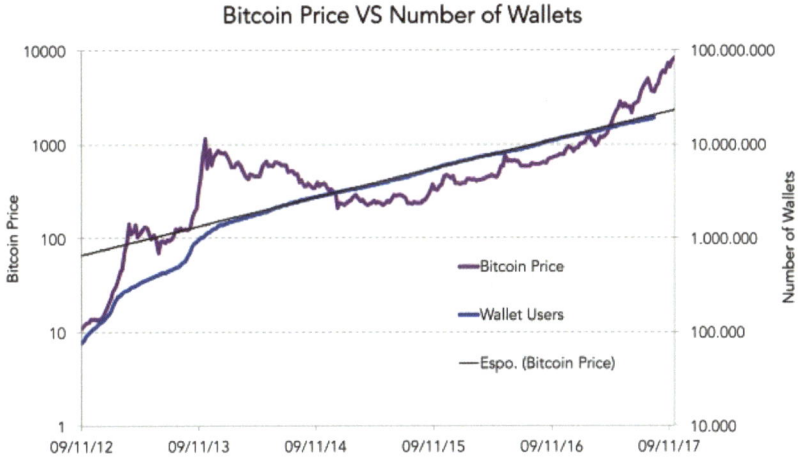

Picture 14 – Bitcoin exponential growth compared with user adoptions

The growth in price is very closely related to the growth rate of people approaching the world of cryptocurrencies and confirms my theory: as long as there are new users entering the world of cryptocurrencies, the price is bound to rise.

For how long? And what will happen then?

At the very least we can gain some understanding from the CMGI stock (whose name and skin by now have changed to ModusLink) in the years following the burst of the New Economy bubble:

Picture 15 – ModusLink bubble crash in 2000-2001

It's impressive to note that, two years after the burst of the internet bubble, the value of the stock returned to just under $10 from over $1,000.

But, if we compare what happened to Bitcoin since the burst of the bubble in December 2017, we notice a substantial difference in performance that allows us to assume that this financial instrument is far from going out of fashion.

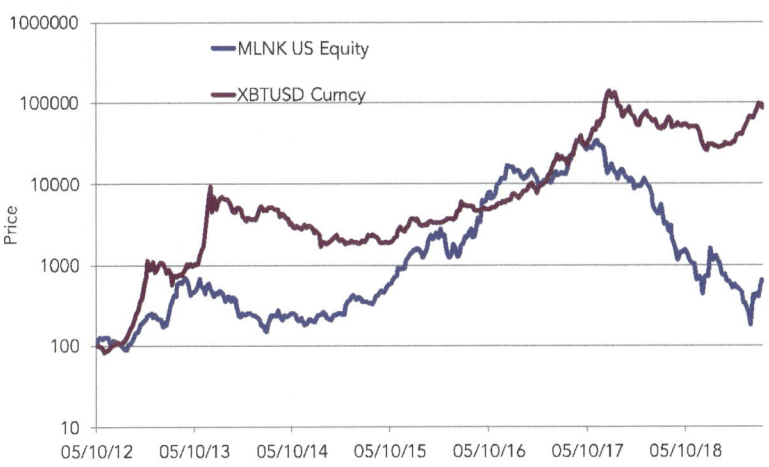

Picture 16 – ModusLink crash VS Bitcoin 2018 crash

RATE OF ADOPTION

It is therefore a question of studying the rate of adoption of cryptocurrencies in the world, to understand where the value of Bitcoin and the cryptocurrency asset class, will go in the future.

Compared to two years ago, the number of open wallets is now at 40 million — almost 0.6% of the earth's population. We can analyze the relationship between wallet opening rate and Bitcoin price as follows:

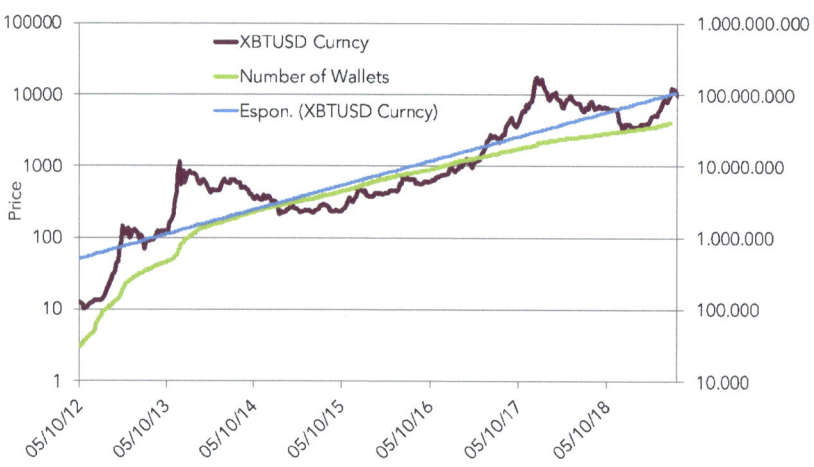

Picture 17 – Wallet and Bitcoin price exponential growth

We can easily see a drop in growth in the number of open wallets which coincides with the burst of the 2018 bubble.

It's interesting to note that, although within the limits that quantities know of the regression tool (which in the graph is exponential since the graph is on a logarithmic scale), the line has slightly risen in slope with respect to the previous graph. This confirms, if it were necessary, that the rise in recent months has in fact accelerated a recovery in the price of Bitcoin compared to the outbreak of the previous crisis in 2013.

Taking these two parameters into consideration, that is, the rate of adoption of number of wallets and exponential line of price-growth, one could hypothesize a Bitcoin price target (which obviously would follow its own path with a very volatile price trend) included between the fork generated by the two trends (assuming that an interest in cryptos doesn't return to pre-crisis exponential rates; I wanted to be prudent).

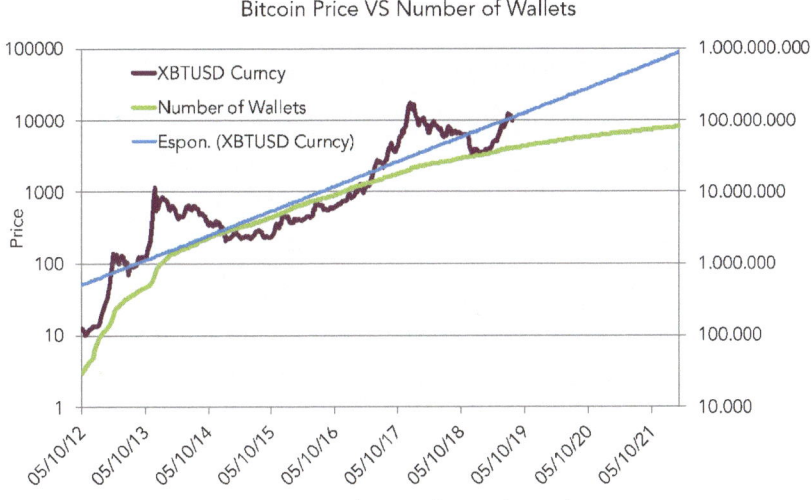

Picture 18 – Price prediction based on these statistics

According to this analysis, we can't exclude that Bitcoin, in the case of continued adoption by the world population (which now stands at 0.6%) can reach a value of $100,000 before the end of 2021.

Clearly, this is a hypothesis. To try to give more structure to the reasoning, I fully report, in the following section, a post I wrote on the topic almost two years ago.

7. THE MONTE CARLO SIMULATION APPLIED TO BITCOIN

I had some fun performing a few Monte Carlo simulations to Bitcoin's historical series in 2017 before the bubble crash, and I reported the entire post here because I believe it is still relevant and can provide to the reader a better comprehension of the Bitcoin phenomena.

Following Bill Gates' proclamation, hypothesizing the price of Bitcoin at $500,000 (in 2017), I tried to understand how this innovative investment asset might behave using classic models, common in the world of traditional finance.
First of all, we need to establish the two parameters required to carry out a Monte Carlo simulation, ie., volatility and average yield.

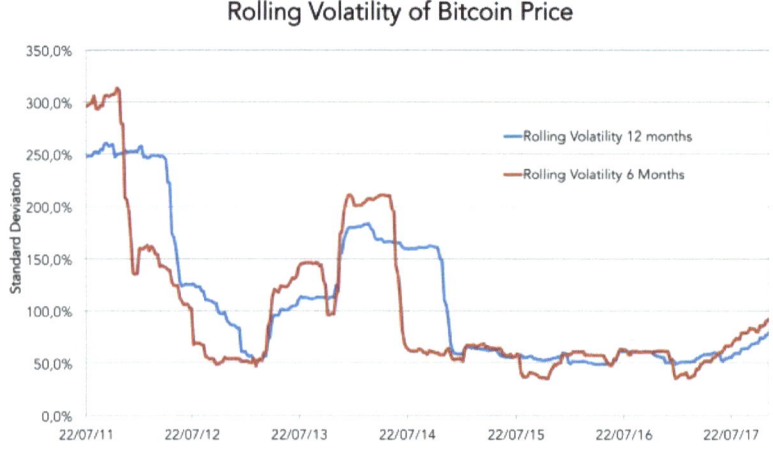

Picture 19 – Rolling volatility during the time

As you can see, the rolling volatility is quite variable, and the average is probably not significant because it's influenced by the early years of Bitcoin, during which the volatility was over 300%.

HOW IT'S READ

The graph is obtained by measuring the twelve-month volatility (blue line) which then moves from week to week, thus determining the trend of the so-called 'rolling' volatility. The same goes for the red line, which is the volatility at six months.

For those who digest historical financial series, high volatility is required for high performance, and Bitcoin is the absolute king of high-yielding time series.

HISTORICAL PERFORMANCE

To use the average yield, I took the line of the exponential graph into consideration (which in reality is a line that grows exponentially on a linear graph.

Picture 20 – Rolling volatility during the time

This line, which in practice is the DIAMAN ratio of the historical Bitcoin series, demonstrates that the average annual return in the long term is an incredible 162%.

Taking the current value of volatility at 12 months, or 79%, and the average of returns +162%, we can perform Monte Carlo simulations (we did 10,000, but we only report 100 to allow for a better graph-viewing experience) to understand where the Bitcoin price behavior could go in the coming months and years.

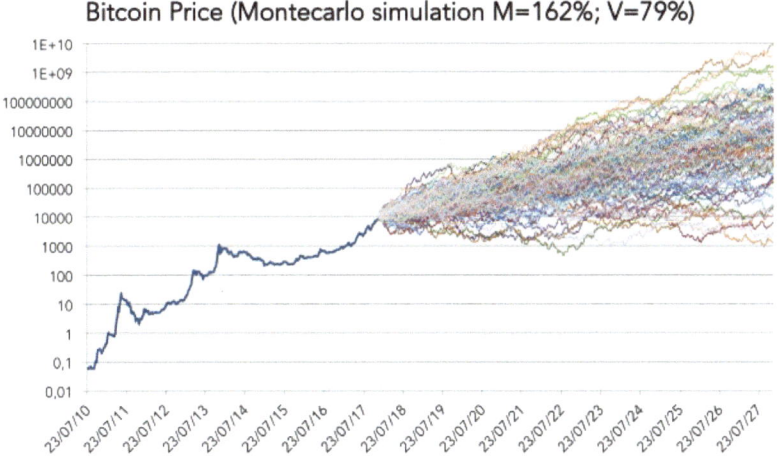

Picture 21 – Monte Carlo simulation on Bitcoin price with historical mean and variance

THE BILLION DOLLAR QUESTION

Is such a trend sustainable in the long-term?

Honestly, it's difficult to believe, even though the intention of the creators of Bitcoin and the logic of scarcity theorize the price of Bitcoin could exceed $500,000 as hypothesized by Bill Gates.

CONSIDERATIONS

The fact that eight decimals have been provided after the comma, allowing the price of Bitcoin to reach a stratospheric value of $100,000,000, may have been the plan of those who created Bitcoin.

HYPOTHESIS

In the happiest of hypotheses, or rather, in the most fortunate simulation among the thousands that were made, it could get there, reaching the expected return and volatility, by 2024.

We're talking about simulations and hypotheses, obviously, which should be supported by an almost absolute diffusion of Bitcoin as a global payment system, difficult to objectively imagine, but still possible from a computational and probabilistic point of view.

PROBABILITY

Looking at the numbers, we could say that there is about a 2% chance that Bitcoin will reach the illusory price of $100 million dollars by 2025.

In order for this Monte Carlo simulation to make sense, we must hypothesize a constant exponential growth in number of users, as explained in the previous paragraph.

VERIFICATION

I've therefore extended the exponential growth of the number of wallets in circulation to date, with an average monthly growth rate of 1.3% (the rate of the last three years).

To argue that the Monte Carlo simulation with average returns equaling 162% and volatility equaling 79% makes sense in the long term, it is necessary to also argue that in 2025 there must be 1.7 billion wallets (which is quite difficult to imagine).

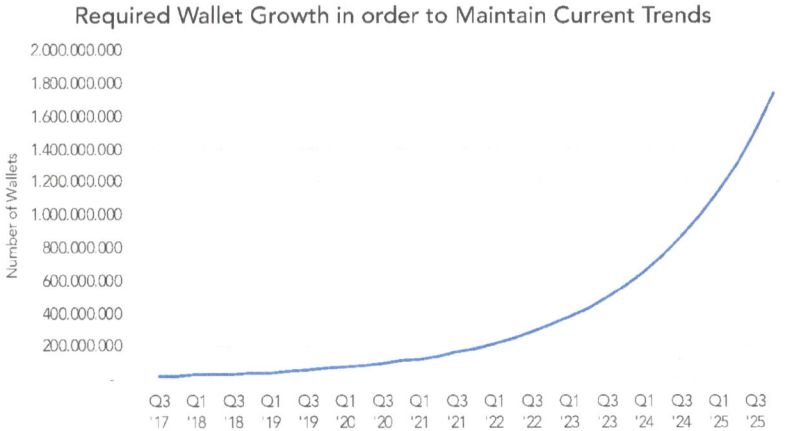

Picture 22 – Number of wallets during the time to maintain actual BTC price trend

OTHER HYPOTHESES

At this point, I thought it more appropriate to reduce the average annual growth over time, so I performed two more simulations. The first assumes a meager 15% annual return (slightly higher than the historical performance of the S&P 500), but arbitrarily keeps the volatility at 79%. The resulting graph is as follows:

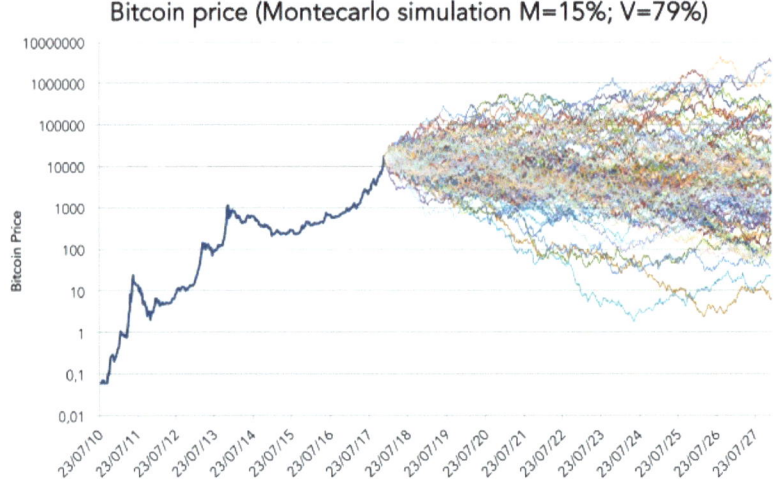

Picture 23 – Monte Carlo simulation with 15% Annual Mean Average

As we can see, it's possible that with such high volatility that bitcoin (even with a probability as low as the previous example of $100 million) could return to the value of a measly $10. But, to honor the real average 10-year results, with a modest average return and high volatility, it is still higher than $110,000.

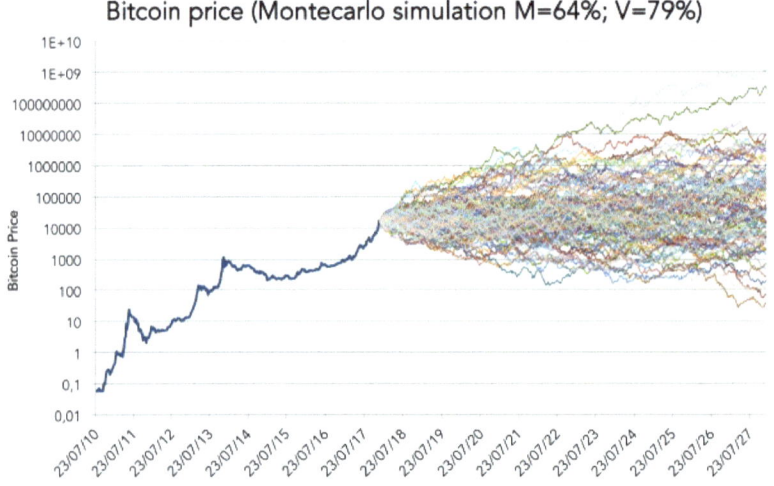

Picture 24 – Monte Carlo simulation with sustainable Sharpe Ratio

Arbitrarily yet, I created a Monte Carlo simulation of 10,000 hypotheses with a much lower average yield than the current one, but adequate to the very high volatility that characterizes Bitcoin. I chose to use an average annual return of 64% and a consistent volatility of 79%.

SUSTAINABLE SHARPE

Why this choice, you may ask yourselves...well, because in all cases I'm curious, and I hope you are too, to see where the price of Bitcoin could go with a Sharpe Index of less than one.

In this hypothesis, there were no cases where the value fell to $10. Not in a single one of the 10,000 simulations.

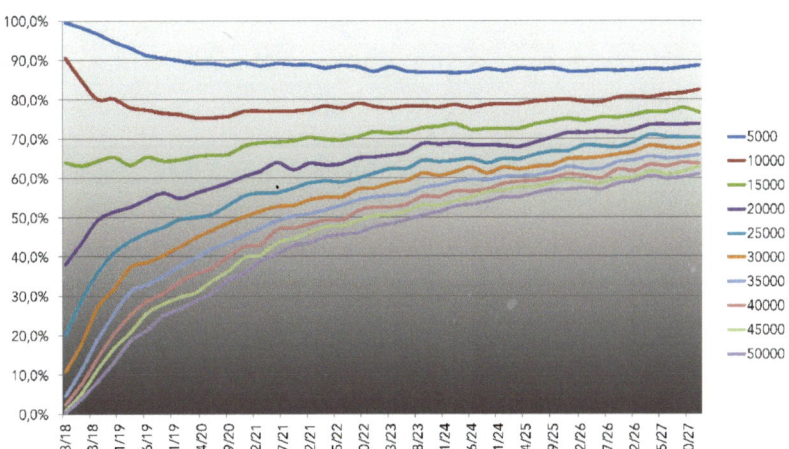

Picture 25 – Probability that the price of Bitcoin will remain above the value during the time

HOW IT'S READ

Is it possible from this simulation to infer the possibility that the price of Bitcoin will be above a determined value? What is the probability that the price of Bitcoin will be above $10,000 in December 2019? From the graph it can be assumed at 77%, which read backwards means that today we have about a 23% chance that in December 2019 the price of Bitcoin will be under $10,000.

POSITIVE

On the contrary, so as not to seem like a bearer of bad luck, what is the possibility that the price of Bitcoin will higher than $50,000 in December 2019? The Monte Carlo simulation said 27% of the random hypotheses with the characteristics described before are worth more than $50,000 in December 2019.

But what is interesting is that there is a 50% probability that the price will be over $50,000 in September of 2023.

TAKE IT WITH A GRAIN OF SALT

The data was obtained from random simulations and we must give them the benefit of the doubt. They are useful to understand the dynamics, potentialities, and the risks that this innovative financial instrument offers.

INNOVATIVE GRAPH

Last but not least, all that remains to be explained is the opening graph of my blog. The Monte Carlo simulations at each trimester offer a distribution of returns deriving from the simulation itself. To describe them as Gaussians, an exponential scale in the X axis must be used, because the resulting distribution is strongly influenced by very high annual average yields, which can make the capitalization effect of returns exponential.

The widest distribution is relative to the end of 2027, while the highest and narrowest green one is relative to the first quarter of 2018. Each subsequent row belongs to the following quarter.

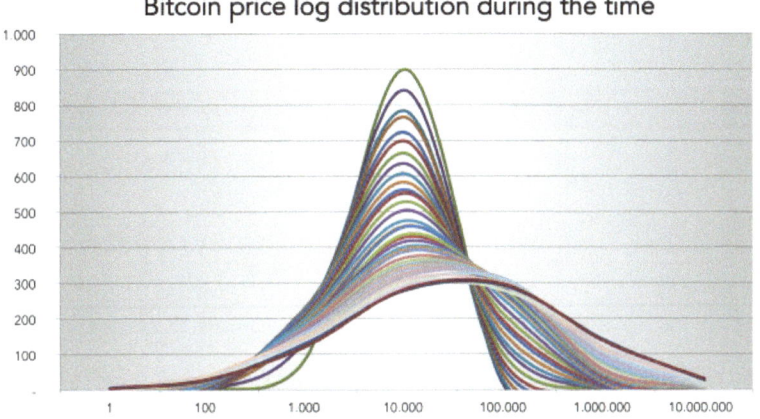

Picture 26 – BTC price log distribution for each quarter

CHAPTER 2 – WHY INVEST CRYPTO ASSETS PROFESSIONALLY

PREFACE: INVESTING IN CRYPTO ASSETS

The path of investing in cryptocurrencies is full of obstacles, ranging from practical (opening a wallet and getting an account on an exchange), to fiscal (no clear rules to follow to declare the profits), to security (password archiving, cold or hard wallet) – just to name a few.

Clearly, when it comes to mass adoption, these problems will have to be solved. I know many start-ups that are working on making the process user friendly just like Wi-Fi on a mobile phone.

But the pitfalls to investing in crypto include high volatility, sudden losses in value, and rapid growth trends. Additionally, you need nerves of steel to withstand uncertainty, and the in-depth knowledge of various projects to avoid so-called *scams*.

To illustrate the importance of having someone professionally manage your crypto investments, below is a graph of losses and recoveries needed to return to initial value.

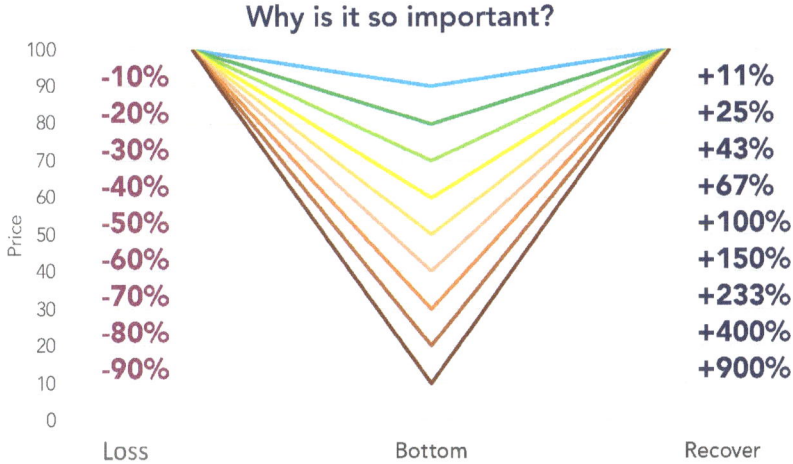

Picture 27 – Difference between losses and returns needed to recover them

To fully understand this, I'll give you two examples. S100,000 on an investment asset that unfortunately loses 50% of its value, and therefore you end up with $50,000 invested in that same asset. How much performance do you have to gain in order to get back to the initial value? 100% — right, you need to double.

But if you lose 90% and you find yourself with $10,000? You'll have to do 900% to get back to $100,000.

Why am I giving you this example?

Because the first 30 cryptocurrencies in 2018 have lost an average of 89%. To return to their initial value, they'd have to make 900% back.

The beauty is that cryptos can do it, but it's easily understandable that if there was someone (even better, a mathematical model) who manages to avoid losing 89%, maybe part of that 900% would be profit and not a recovery of previous losses.

The second risk is finding yourself with $10,000 in the account due to crypto volatility, having no professional support alongside, and deciding to close the investment before losing everything, doing much greater damage in the process. Believe me, this is by far the greatest risk in these investments.

In this chapter we'll explore the reasons and advantages of investing in crypto assets through an investment vehicle rather than relying on DIY. Even if you have experience in financial markets, the world of crypto is different and a lack of experience could cost you a great deal of money.

8. THE ADVANTAGE OF QUANTITATIVE MODELS

Quantitative models are investment processes based on more or less complex rules that are rigorously applied, often through automated buying or selling processes.
With the onset of increasingly powerful computers and access to even simpler software to use, quantitative models are gaining more and more popularity with asset manager at every level.

Many studies, such as Faber's paper A Quantitative Approach to Tactical Asset Allocation show that quantitative models are valid choices when, for example, timing the market,

Without trying to write a thesis on quantitative models, one of the most famous models is the one based on *Trend Following* logic, or rather, entering and exiting the markets by watching trends.

DIAMAN was one of the first companies in Italy to use these models dating back to 2002, with excellent results on behalf of institutional wealth management clients.

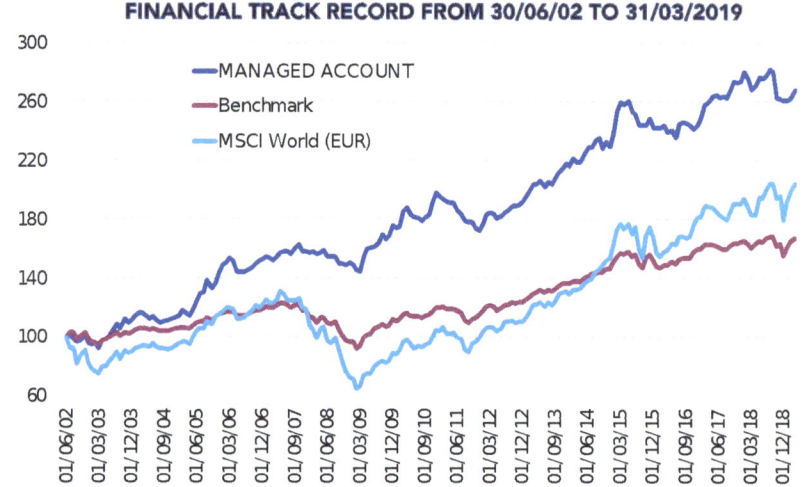

Picture 28 – Real managed account track record compared with MSCI World

The above graph shows how the management of a well-known Italian bank, of which DIAMAN was the advisor since June 2002, significantly outperformed both the benchmark (a balanced portfolio) and the MSCI World, by greatly reducing losses in the years 2002 and 2008 during two major financial market crises.

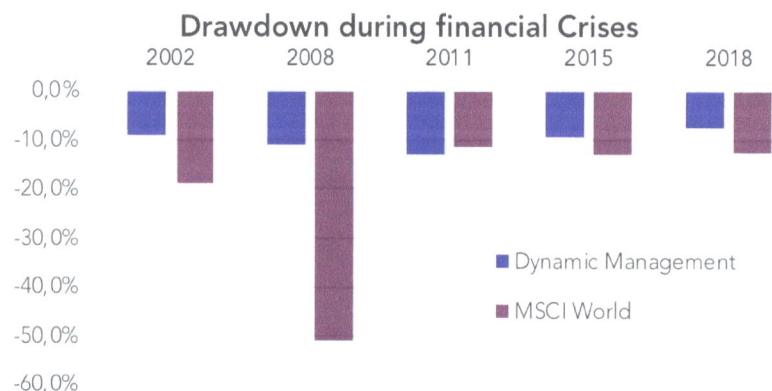

Picture 29 – Maximum drawdown suffered by the managed account and MSCI World

From an investor's point of view, investment risk is perceived during market downturn, as the average investor doesn't know how to interpret nor estimate the volatility. Therefore, the drawdown is fundamental to correctly assess the risks of a strategy.

In addition to loss over a period of time, from an investor's point of view, recovery time is important to getting back to the previous maximum i.e., how long should the investor be in apnea to wait for new highs.

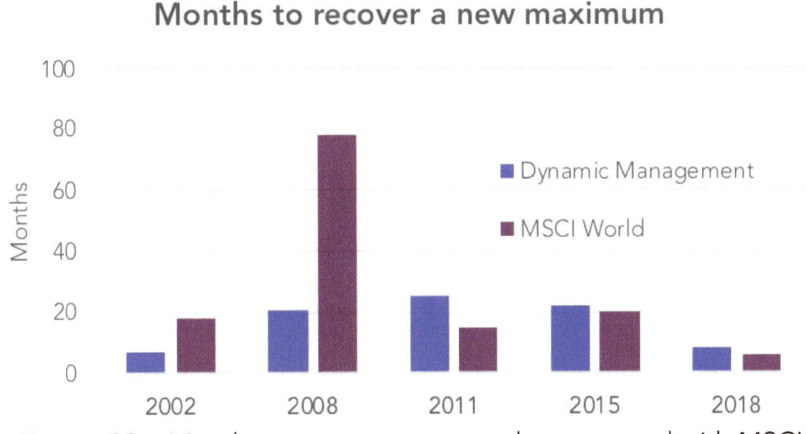

Picture 30 – Months to return to new peaks compared with MSCI World

From these two graphs it is clear that using Trend Following logic to enter and exit financial markets is essential to give customers lower risk expectations and less time to recover previous losses.

In the world of crypto assets, where volatility is more than four times the volatility of the stock market, the use of trend following models is fundamental, as we will see in the next paragraph.

In the meantime, I'd like to focus on a document by PwC, a well-known business consulting firm that analyzed the hedge fund market in a crypto asset investment context.

While Bitcoin lost more than 70% of its value in 2018, the average hedge fund based on fundamental or discretionary approaches managed to contain only a small part of the bear market losses. Quantitative hedge funds, on the other hand, were able to obtain positive returns.

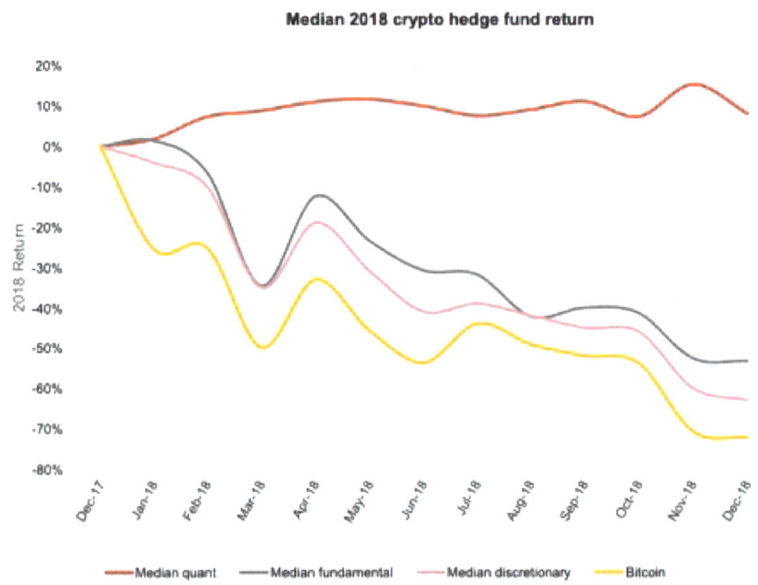

Picture 31 –PwC chart regarding crypto hedge fund Industry track record in 2018

This analysis reinforces our conviction that it's essential to invest in this asset class using a more scientific approach, both to risk less, but of course to have a greater chance of earning.

This is why we developed a *Market Timing* strategy which we'll explain in the next paragraph.

9. MARKET TIMING WITH CRYPTO

We've been using our timing model mechanism for several months to manage a real portfolio of ten of the main cryptocurrencies currently on the market. Before describing that model, I'll share a post written on June 2018 regarding the use of one of our proprietary indicators to enter and exit Bitcoin.

A few years ago, I explained how to perform market timing using the DIAMAN Ratio as a predictive indicator of market trends.

I applied the DIAMAN Ratio to cryptocurrencies to check if the digital asset class could work and have a practical use.

To my great surprise, (though I was actually expecting it), without any kind of optimization, I discovered that the DIAMAN Ratio is able to achieve better yields than the cryptocurrencies themselves, thus reducing maximum losses.

Why did I expect it? Because market timing works great in times of market crisis, for example in 2003 and 2008. Those who benefited from our models lost much less in comparison to the market, thereby obtaining a risk adjusted performance (performance adjusted for the risk assumed) that was significantly better than the buy and hold strategy (buying and always remaining invested).

MARKET TIMING VS. BUY & HOLD

Many contend that the buy and hold methodology is superior to a timing strategy, but I am convinced that our job is to reduce risks for the investor and help them avoid losses, even if only temporarily, of large sums of money. As Murphy's law implies, the customer needs money just when markets go wrong.

It's natural for things to be this way, just as it is natural that when you drop a slice of bread and jam, it always falls face-down (due to its differential weight). It's normal for an entrepreneur to need money when the markets go down because he's no longer receiving dividends from the companies (for example).

PROS & CONS

In times of market growth, market timing struggles in returning the same stock market returns because of false signals, but it's the price you pay precisely to avoid big losses that sometimes can happen with the markets.

Over the course of the last 16 years we've developed strong experience and robust models to do market timing on stock market assets, as well as a statistical indicator called the DIAMAN Ratio, which was presented at several international conferences and published in Wilmott Magazine in 2014.

The DIAMAN Ratio works as a trend indicator, so if it's positive it means there's a positive trend. If it's close to zero it means there's no clear trend, and if it's negative, it obviously means it's better not to invest in that asset.

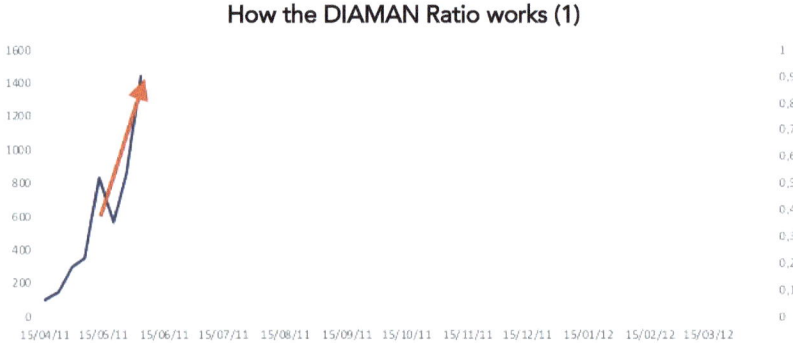

Picture 32 – Example of DIAMAN Ratio calculation for a historical series (1)

As an example, I took the price of Bitcoin during an unsuspecting era, in this case, April 2011, when Bitcoin rose sharply on a very clear trend.

The DIAMAN Ratio at one month in this case was clearly positive, therefore the signal was to invest in Bitcoin, which allowed us to benefit from the strong price increase.

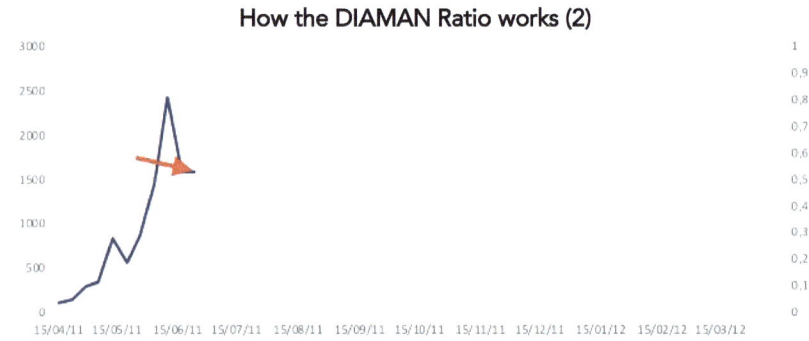

Picture 33 – Example of DIAMAN Ratio calculation; negative trend (2)

Then the price quickly went back down from the highs and the DIAMAN Ratio, after one month, rapidly turned to zero and became negative. At that point, the signal to sell was triggered.

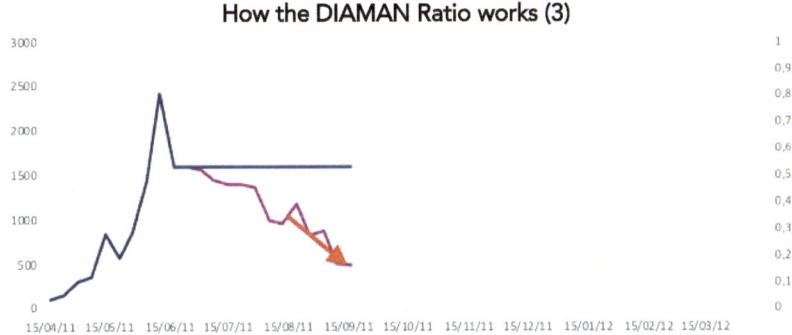

Picture 34 – Example of DIAMAN Ratio calculation; negative trend (3)

This signal was then confirmed in the following months, where Bitcoin suffered a decline, and the DIAMAN Ratio, being negative, continued to indicate to remain out of the market.

This activity, carried out with determination and continuity over time, leads to riding the positive waves of crypto asset trends that are often incredibly profitable in a short time. This way manages to avoid, even with some inevitable false signals, the negative trends that in some cases brought the price of Bitcoin to lose up to 90% of its value.

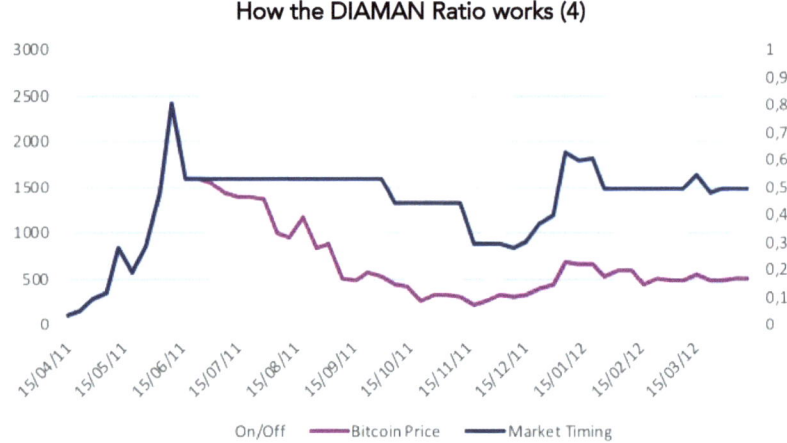

Picture 35 – Example of track record thanks to the DIAMAN Ratio

The reason I expected timing on crypto assets to be profitable is due to the enormous volatility and resilience of this particular asset class.

As explained in several posts regarding drawdown, such as Deterministic Indicator of Maximum Loss, an 80% loss requires a recovery of 400% to return to its initial value, so it's sufficient to stop the loss at 50% to have an advantage over the buy and hold, despite slightly less than perfect entry times.

The Bitcoin historical series proves it, because in its nine years of life, there have been a variety of opportunities for entering and exiting — as well as false signals. But, if you look at the long term, the performance obtained through market timing, thanks to the DIAMAN Ratio, was greatly superior to the already incredible Bitcoin performance.

Picture 36 – Back test using the DR on bitcoin price (log scale)

If we then consider the reduction in volatility and the risk taken (maximum drawdown went from 91% to 65%), the so-called Risk Adjusted Performance is clearly in favor of market timing. The evidence is seen through the Sharpe Ratio and the relationship between DIAMAN Ratio and Ulcer Index.

	Market Timing	Bitcoin
Total Return	47298716%	11770046%
Annual Return	437,6%	349,4%
MaxDD	-65,5%	-91,4%
UI	0,263	0,515
Volatility	120,8%	134,1%
Sharpe Ratio	3,622	2,605
DIAMAN Ratio	2,571	1,743
DR/UI	9,782	3,387

Table 1 – Comparative statistics between market timing and buy and hold on BTC

We can therefore confirm that using a *risk-on* or *risk-off* indicator allows us to obtain better returns than the underlying security (just like with the stock market) by reducing maximum drawdown, volatility, and increasing efficiency (Sharpe Ratio and DIAMAN Ratio).

This happens because Bitcoin and crypto asset trends, in general, are both marked by sharp highs and lows, allowing for the use of quantitative trend following models such as the DIAMAN Ratio.

MULTI-FORMULA MODEL

When it came to our strategy, we decided to abide by the following investment process:

1) For each crypto, five different quantitative models indicate whether IN or OUT.
2) An investment committee using artificial intelligence decides whether IN or OUT based on the number of IN models (this number may vary based on different factors).
3) An algorithmic trading model spreads the purchase or sale orders across five different exchanges with variable order sizes to reduce the impact on the price of the single crypto.

For those who wish to obtain more information on the models adopted, they can request an appointment at our offices in Malta by writing an email to pm@diaman.partners where they will receive information on our models.

10. WHY DIAMAN STARTS WITH AN ADVANTAGE

DIAMAN is a company that was founded in 2002 by Daniele Bernardi to offer investment models based on quantitative processes to its institutional clients.

The company has always invested well over 10% of its turnover every year on the research and development of indicators and quantitative models, useful for facing financial markets, reducing real risk for investors, and creating specific strategies at the request of customers.
Over the years, various academic papers written by our team have been published in industry specific journals concerning statistical indicators such as the DIAMAN Ratio. Additionally, we've published on investment methodologies such as the Target Strategy and Return Parity Approach, and have proposed new probabilistic financial market analysis approaches as seen in The Right Time to Enter.

All these works were carried out thanks to collaborations with university professors from the Universities of Siena, Padua, Venice and Milan.

Aware that innovation also means education, dating back to 2005, the company has organized international events for the dissemination of quantitative methodologies. These events have boasted keynote speeches by international level speakers such as Paul Wilmott, John Hiatt, Edward Altman, Andrew Kumiega and many others.

To increase the spread of quantitative models among industry operators as well as to increase financial culture in Italy, the company also purchased a significant share of Investor's Magazine Italy, which circulates information and financial markets methodologies on a bi-monthly basis.

For these reasons, and combined with a track record of results obtained over time, DIAMAN is in a position of advantage over many competitors to create an effectively profitable quantitative strategy regarding crypto assets. Consequently, we can manage an alternative fund with quantitative models and excellent potential for returns.

11. BACKTEST AND REAL TRACK RECORD

Investing in crypto assets may reveal itself to be the wrong bet — but, it could also be a huge win. It certainly was a winner for those who approached this asset class in 2015 and garnered incredible annual returns.

Using a risk-on/risk-off approach, that is, market timing on the stock markets, means having to compromise some returns during positive markets due to false signals. However, it makes it possible to reduce losses considerably in case the markets turn highly negative.

Crypto assets trends are much more obvious, so any false signals are more than offset by the remarkable performance that the market is able to generate afterward.
Consider, for example, that from January to July 2019, BTC tripled its value from 2018 lows. So, an active approach has the ability of recovering losses reaching 50% of their value in a relatively short time.

We simulated a basket of ten crypto assets, attributing greater importance to the crypto assets with greater liquidity and capitalization size, and weighted it according to proprietary logic.

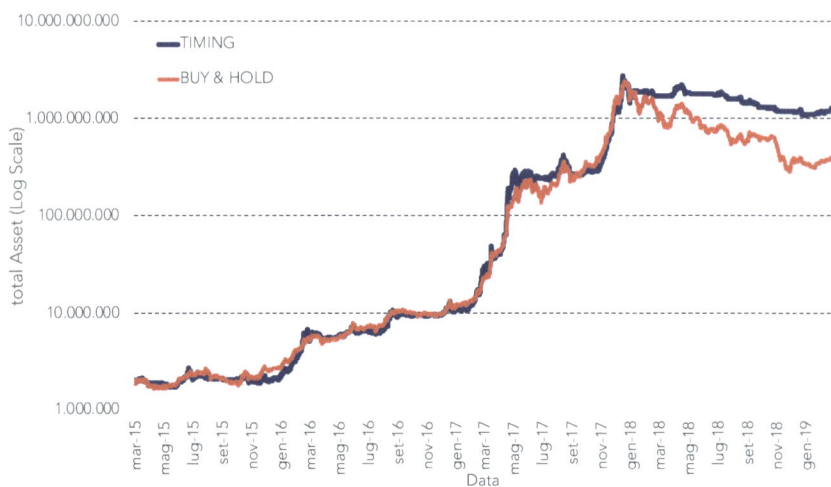

Picture 37 – Back test with multi-strategies and AI on a basket of ten cryptos

As you will note, if we had started a fund for $20 million in March 2015 with our quantitative model, today the fund would be worth almost $20 billion. With a buy and hold strategy, the fund would still have generated a considerable $4 billion in value.

Of course, hindsight is twenty-twenty, but regardless, this volatile asset class remains intact today with the same potential for future growth. If we look at this table analysis, we see the incredible returns made in only four years:

STATISTICAL INDICATORS	TIMING	BUY & HOLD
PERFORMANCE	97805%	19764%
ANNUAL PERFORMANCE	470%	289%
STANDARD DEVIATION	81.67%	77.76%
MAX DRAWDOWN	-52.92%	-88.40%

Table 2 – Principal statistics of the timing strategies and buy & hold on ten cryptos

These very interesting numbers show that our models were able to greatly reduce the risk of maximum loss (though a 50% loss is significant for a common investor). Additionally, they prompted us to invest personal money last fall to verify the validity of the models using the same basket of ten cryptos from the back test.

Picture 38 – Real track record of a managed account using the multi-strategies and AI with respect to a buy and hold basket of ten cryptos

As of October 2018, the crypto basket lost 60% of its value. Yet, thanks to our model, we managed to contain the loss of the period to 22%, resulting in greater ease of returning to initial value, and eventually exceeding it.

This advantage has translated into an over performance that we are still maintaining with respect to a buy and hold strategy, confirming that active management on a quantitative basis can both protect the investment and obtain higher-than-average returns.

12. THE IMPORTANCE OF LIQUIDITY

Many years ago, probably in 2007, Prof. Francesco Corielli, professor of quantitative finance at Bocconi University in Milan, said to me, *"volatility is the price you pay to be able to liquidate your investments every day."*

If you think about the value of your home, you have the perception that it won't change over time, or at most that it increases or decreases very gradually. Truthfully, you only discover the real value of your home when you sell it, but if there was an iPad in front of your home, where every passerby could write his purchase offer every day, you'd discover that the price of the house every day was different based on who passed by and their perception of the value of your home.

The lesson is that volatility is essential to also obtain great returns.

It's impossible to have a return of 10% or even 100% with a volatility of zero. **The higher the expected return, the higher the volatility must be**. For this reason, when we created an alternative fund for crypto at DIAMAN, we made sure to implement a weekly NAV.

An investor, whether the fund is going wrong or extraordinarily well, must have the option to carry out the investment with very high frequency. In a month's time, the crypto market might double — or half. In our opinion, it isn't right to obligate investors to take this risk when they decide to invest, or lose opportunities when they decide to disinvest.

The weekly NAV, though it means more work for the fund administrator and the management company, is fundamental to invest in this asset class with good control over the fund's performance. With the NAV, we also have the possibility of liquidating the investment quickly.

13. CORRELATIONS BETWEEN ASSET CLASSES

Those who are familiar with the history of DIAMAN also know that we give little importance to the concept of correlation, especially within the asset class itself.

To imagine that investing in American stocks, versus Japanese or European stocks, lowers the portfolio's risk because the past has shown to have few correlations is utopian. Typically, within an asset class, there is little correlation when things go well. That's often due to the investment strategies of large active funds that take different investment factors into consideration. When things go wrong, correlation tends to go to one because everything goes down.

To be really efficient, I would need the opposite to happen i.e., that correlations go towards one when markets rise, and zero or negative when markets fall. Conversely, if I were to analyze different investment asset classes such as equity, bonds, and commodities, the use of correlations is different.

So, we analyzed the correlations at one week and one month for these asset classes compared to Bitcoin. The purpose was to evaluate an anticipated effect from the inclusion of this asset class within an asset allocation.

Weekly Correlation	XBT-USD Cross Rate	S&P 500 INDEX	US Generic Govt 10 Year Yield	BBG Commodity	TOPIX Index (TOKYO)
XBT-USD Cross Rate	1,000	0,037	- 0,048	0,071	0,016
S&P 500 INDEX	0,037	1,000	0,293	0,359	0,606
US Generic Govt 10 Year Yield	- 0,048	0,293	1,000	0,162	0,385
BBG Commodity	0,071	0,359	0,162	1,000	0,289
TOPIX Index (TOKYO)	0,016	0,606	0,385	0,289	1,000

Table 3 – Weekly correlation between principal asset classes

From this graph it can be seen that the dollar price of bitcoin on a weekly basis is virtually unrelated to any traditional asset class.

Technically, the longer the observation period, the more likely positive correlations would emerge. For this reason, we performed the correlation analysis on a monthly basis.

Monthly Correlation	XBT-USD Cross Rate	S&P 500 INDEX	US Generic Govt 10 Year Yield	BBG Commodity	TOPIX INDEX (TOKYO)
XBT-USD Cross Rate	1,000	0,076	- 0,137	0,099	0,158
S&P 500 INDEX	0,076	1,000	0,300	0,465	0,738
US Generic Govt 10 Year Yield	- 0,137	0,300	1,000	0,153	0,611
BBG Commodity	0,099	0,465	0,153	1,000	0,302
TOPIX INDEX (TOKYO)	0,158	0,738	0,611	0,302	1,000

Table 4 – Monthly correlation between principal asset classes

In this case as well, correlations between bitcoin price and other asset classes are not very pronounced. This is a very strong point in favor of including investments in crypto assets within a strategic asset allocation, especially with active management.
In the next section, we'll analyze the appropriate percentage of crypto assets to include within an asset allocation.

14. INVEST WITH HOMEOPATHIC DOSES

Risk finance techniques are often adopted with a risk budget associated to each asset class based on the volatility of the underlying market.

The first to propose such logic was Edward Qian in his 2005 white paper *Efficient Portfolios Through True Diversification*. Clearly, an asset class like crypto, with a volatility of 80%, must be allocated cautiously.

I do believe that the time has come to speak about risk/opportunity instead of expected risk/return. Similarly, it's time to start inserting a small dose of crypto assets in the portfolio owing to incredible opportunity. That becomes more apparent in an era such as our current one, where 40% of bonds in the world have negative returns — and many stock markets have been at their highest with a growth trend that has lasted for many years.

Imagine for a moment that in March 2015, you'd purchased 5% of a basket of ten crypto assets and that you included it in an investment portfolio. You also left the remaining 95% in cash with no return.

Below, you'll see the performance of your investment portfolio compared to the S&P 500 Index.

Picture 39 – Simulation of a portfolio 95% cash and 5% in a basket of crypto assets vs. 100% invested in S&P 500 Index

If you had invested €95,000 in cash and €5,000 in this crypto basket, you would have returned €488,000 to your client at the end of June 2019.

Fantastic, isn't it? Had we not stopped there, the customer in December 2017 would have had about €2.7 million — and I don't think they would have been very happy to find themselves with less than a fifth of its maximum value.

We've been in finance for over 20 years, and these figures make our head. But, as I explained in the first chapter of this e-book, not only did they happen, there are many chances they will repeat in the future.

So, we've adopted a very simple strategy:

1) Invest 5% of a client's portfolio in crypto.

2) Whenever 10% of weight is exceeded in the portfolio, it is sold and brought back to 5% of the value of the portfolio.
3) If the weight of the crypto in the portfolio falls below 5% at the end of the month, an additional 0.5% of crypto is brought back in.

This simple strategy allows you to maintain crypto risk exposure at 5% and therefore reduce the risk of a very contained drawdown. Throughout, you'll maintain some very interesting potentials for return.

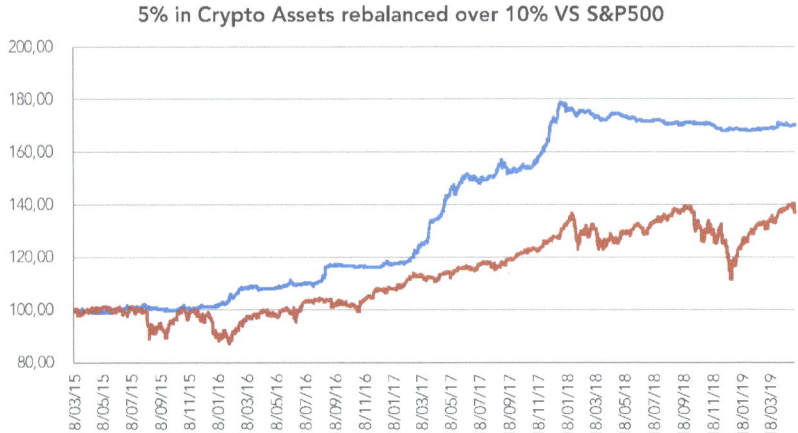

Picture 40 – Simulation of a portfolio with 5% in crypto assets with automatic rebalanced each time arrive to 10% of exposure, against 100% invested in S&P 500 Index

By keeping the crypto asset class within the ranges of 5% and 10% of the client's investment portfolio, the total return on the portfolio is almost double that of the S&P 500 in recent years, with a volatility and drawdown that is two thirds lower.

Statistical Indicators	Asset Allcoation: 985% Cash + 5%-10% in Crypto	S&P 500 Index
Total Return	70,229%	37,1479%
Annual Return	13,513%	7,8166%
Standard Deviation	5,067%	13,4295%
Maximum Drawdown	-6,144%	-19,7782%

Table 5 – Principal statistical results of the example

Since the correlation of Bitcoin to the S&P 500 is equal to 0.02, we can easily note that a homeopathic dose of asset allocation is desirable to find a source of yield, that is at least supplemental.

For those who are interested, we've prepared an Excel spreadsheet with the tree parameters described above to help simulate the correct percentages to be included in a portfolio based on the customer's risk characteristics.

To receive a copy, send an email to marketing@diaman.partners and the file will be sent to the email address requesting it.

CONCLUSIONS

DIAMAN Partners has become the delegated manager for a notified alternative investment fund based in Malta. This fund will invest indirectly in crypto assets.

Since this document is open to a broad audience and it isn't possible to ensure its all readers are qualified or professional investors, DIAMAN Partners prefers not to describe the fund's characteristics.

If you are a qualified or professional investor, you can request more information regarding the alternative fund by sending an email to marketing@diaman.partners with the subject line *request more information.* If you are a retail investor, you can access this type of investment through the www.openphinance.com digital investment platform. Once there, you can ask for more information by sending an email to marketing@diaman.partners.

BIBLIOGRAPHY

- Satoshi Nakamoto (2009). Bitcoin White Paper: *A Peer-to-Peer Electronic Cash System*
- Buterin, Vitalik (2013). Ethereum White Paper: A next-generation smart contract and decentralized application platform
- DIAMAN Capital (2018). The PHI Token White Paper
- Daniele Bernardi and Ruggero Bertelli (2014): The DIAMAN Ratio
- Daniele Bernardi and Ruggero Bertelli (2016): The Return Parity Approach
- Daniele Bernardi and Ruggero Bertelli (2016): Target Strategy: A Practical Application to ETFs and ETCs
- Francesco Canella, Tiziano Vargiolu e Enrico Edoli (2013): The Right Time to Enter
- Mebane Faber (2013), A Quantitative Approach to Tactical Asset Allocation
- Edward Qian (2005): Efficient portfolios through true diversification
- Didier Sornette (2018): Are Bitcoin Bubbles Predictable? Combining a Generalized Metcalfe's Law and the LPPLS Model
- Didier Sornette (2018): Can We Use Volatility to Diagnose Financial Bubbles? Lessons from 40 Historical Bubbles
- Didier Sornette (2010): Bubbles Everywhere in Human Affairs

DISCLAIMER

This document regarding Crypto Assets is intended for informational purposes only and in no way can be considered promotional material by DIAMAN Partners, nor is it intended for distribution.

Crypto Assets may be affected by oscillations in currency exchange rates thereby affecting any investment return. If you invest in Crypto Assets you may lose some or all of the money you invest. The value of your investment may go down as well as up.

Any information shown in this e-book is not related to any product or financial service.

Any potential investors looking to invest in an Alternative Investment Fund related to this kind of Asset Class should refer to the offering documentation of the fund and consult with their respective independent financial and tax advisors. Investment decisions should be made exclusively by independent assessment on the basis of the investor's financial position and investment objectives, as well as the investor's personal interpretation together with the fund's offering documentation.

BIOGRAPHY

Born in 1969, Automotive Engineer, Daniele Bernardi is a serial-entrepreneur constantly searching for innovation. Chairman of DIAMAN Sicav and CEO of DIAMAN, a Group dedicated to the development of profitably investment strategies, Bernardi's activity is oriented to the development of mathematic models, which simplify investors and family offices decision making processes, for risk reduction. He is the author of interesting academic papers about innovation in finance, published by Wilmott Magazine in May 2014 and on Journal of Accounting and Finance in April 2015. Models, indexes, and indicators developed by Bernardi have been presented in international conferences such as the Financial Management Association Conference in Denver and Nashville, the World Financial Conference in Shanghai, Venice and New York. Bernardi is also Charman of Investors' Magazine Italia SRL and DIAMAN Tech SRL and CEO of DIAMAN Partners; He was recognized as "Inventor" by European Patent office for his European and Russian Patent into mobile payment field.

www.ingramcontent.com/pod-product-compliance
Lightning Source LLC
Chambersburg PA
CBHW040321220526